Celebrate Winter

All About
Winter
Weather

by Kathryn Clay

Raintree is an imprint of Capstone Global Library Limited, a company incorporated in England and Wales having its registered office at 7 Pilgrim Street, London, EC4V 6LB – Registered company number: 6695582

www.raintree.co.uk
myorders@raintree.co.uk

Text © Capstone Global Library Limited 2016
The moral rights of the proprietor have been asserted.

Editorial Creditss
Erika L. Shores, editor; Cynthia Della-Rovere, designer;
Tracy Cummins, media researcher; Tori Abraham, production specialist

ISBN 978 1 4747 0312 3 (hardback)
19 18 17 16 15
10 9 8 7 6 5 4 3 2 1

ISBN 978 1 4747 0317 8 (paperback)
20 19 18 17 16 15
10 9 8 7 6 5 4 3 2 1

British Library Cataloguing in Publication Data
A full catalogue record for this book is available from the British Library.

Photo Credits
Dreamstime: Robin Van Olderen, 12, SandraRBarba, 6—7, Smellme, 16 (right); Newscom: ZUMA Press/Tony Crocetta, 26—27; Shutterstock: Aaron Amat, 27 (top), ala737, 13 (bottom), Alta Oosthuizen, 15 (top), 18, Ana Gram, 25, 29 (inset), bjogroet, 11 (top), Black Sheep Media (grass), throughout, Chantal de Bruijne (African landscape), back cover and throughout, creative, 10, e2dan, 13 (top), Eric Isselee, cover, back cover, 1, 4, 7 (top), 11 (bottom), 21 (top), 23 (top), 32, Gerrit_de_Vries, 14 (top), 17, Jez Bennett, 14 (bottom), John Michael Evan Potter, 9, Maggy Meyer, 28—29, MattiaATH, 8, Mogens Trolle, 15 (bottom), moizhusein, 20—21, 23, Moments by Mullineux, 5, Sean Stanton, 19, Serge Vero, 24, Stuart G. Porter, 22

Contents

Hello, winter

Grab a coat.

Put on a hat.

Winter is here!

The air gets colder.

Snowflakes start to fall.

Plants don't grow.

Trees are bare.

Frost covers branches.

Some places stay warm.

Snow doesn't fall.

People wear shorts all year.

Ice and snow

Brrr! The air is cold.

Rain freezes.

Frozen rain is called sleet.

Roads are icy.

Gritters keep roads safe.

They spread salt and sand.

Wind blows snow
all around.

It's a blizzard.

Winter fun

Lakes can freeze.

Molly goes ice fishing.

Jack plays ice hockey.

Sophia makes a snowman.

Lily and Layla go sledging.

What will you do in the winter?

Glossary

bare not covered

blizzard snowstorm with high winds making it difficult to see

freeze turn from liquid (water) to solid (ice)

frost layer of ice crystals formed on the ground or other surfaces

gritter vehicle that spreads sand and salt onto roads to melt snow and ice

winter one of the four seasons of the year; winter is after autumn and before spring

Read more

Snow (Weather Wise), Helen Cox-Cannons
(Raintree, 2014)

Weather Infographics (Infographics), Chris Oxlade
(Raintree, 2014)

Websites

www.naturedetectives.org.uk/winter/
Download winter wildlife ID sheets, pick up some great
snowy-weather-game ideas and discover all the fun you
can have with winter sticks!

www.wildlifewatch.org.uk/
Explore the Wildlife Trust's wildlife watch website and
get busy this winter spotting interesting winter plants and
animals living near by! Follow badger's blog for great
wildlife spotting tips and some fascinating photographs.

Index